D1518277

DISCOVERING CAREERS FOR YOUR FUTURE

advertising & marketing

Ferguson
An imprint of ☑® Facts On File

Discovering Careers for Your Future: Advertising & Marketing

Ferguson
An imprint of Facts On File, Inc.
132 West 31st Street
New York NY 10001

Discovering careers for your future. Advertising & marketing
      p. cm.
Includes index.
    ISBN 0-8160-5847-4 (hc : alk. paper)
    1. Advertising—Vocational guidance—Juvenile literature. 2. Marketing—Vocational guidance—Juvenile literature. I. J.G. Ferguson Publishing Company
Publishing Company.
    HF5828.4.D57 2005
    658.8'0023—dc22   2005003300

Contents

Introduction

You may not have decided yet what you want to be in the future. And you don't have to decide right away. You do know that right now you are interested in advertising and marketing. Do any of the statements below describe you? If so, you may want to begin thinking about what a career in advertising and marketing might mean for you.

___I like to write songs or stories.
___I like to perform research.
___I enjoy public speaking.
___I like to listen to or record sounds and music.
___I enjoy watching or listening to commercials.
___I enjoy photography.
___I spend a lot of time using art, illustration, or video-editing programs on my computer.
___I enjoy statistics and mathematics.
___I enjoy art or illustration.
___I like to create and give surveys to my friends and family.
___I enjoy fashion.
___I like to arrange and present products at garage and yard sales.
___I enjoy informing others about a new band I've heard or product that I've purchased.

Discovering Careers for Your Future: Advertising & Marketing is a book about careers in advertising and marketing, from advertising account executives to illustrators to public opinion researchers. Careers in this field can be found in business offices, in radio and television stations, in recording studios, in department stores, in photography studios, and in production houses. While the advertising and marketing industry is primarily located in large cities such as New York and Los Angeles, positions are available throughout the United States and the world.

This book describes many possibilities for future careers in advertising and marketing. Read through it and see how the different careers are connected. For example, if you are interested in writing or composing, you should read the articles on composers, copywriters, and other entries in this book. If you are interested in working in an artistic position, you will want to read about art directors, fashion illustrators and photographers, graphic designers, and other careers. If you want to manage people or business accounts, you will want to read about advertising account executives, advertising and marketing managers, and other careers. If gathering information sounds exciting, you will want to read about demographers, marketing research analysts, public opinion researchers, and other careers. Go ahead and explore!

As you read through the careers in this book, you will notice that each article features answers to the following questions:

What Do Advertising and Marketing Workers Do?

The first section of each chapter begins with a heading such as "What Advertising and Marketing Managers Do" or "What Photo Stylists Do." This section tells what it's like to work at this job. It also describes typical responsibilities and working conditions. Which workers are employed on fashion shoots? Which ones work at computers in offices? Which ones work in design studios? This section answers these and other questions.

How Do I Become an Advertising and Marketing Worker?

The section called "Education and Training" tells you what schooling you need for employment in each job—a high school diploma, training at a junior college, a college degree, or more. It also talks about what high school and college courses you should take to prepare for the field.

How Much Do Advertising and Marketing Workers Earn?

The "Earnings" section gives salary figures for the job described in the chapter. These figures give you a general idea of how much money people with this job can make. Keep in mind that many people really earn more or less than the amounts given here because actual salaries depend on many different things, such as the size of the company, the location of the company, and the amount of education, training, and experience you have. Generally, but not always, larger companies located in major cities pay more than smaller ones in smaller cities and towns, and people with more education, training, and experience earn more. Also remember that these figures are current or recent salaries. They will probably be different by the time you are ready to enter the workforce.

What Is the Future of Advertising and Marketing Careers?

The "Outlook" section discusses the employment outlook for the career: whether the total number of people employed in this career will increase or decrease in the coming years and whether jobs in this field will be easy or hard to find. These predictions are based on economic conditions, the size and makeup of the population, foreign competition, and new technology. Terms such as "faster than the average," "about as fast as the average," and "slower than the average" are used by the U.S. Department of Labor to describe job growth predicted by government data.

Keep in mind that these predictions are general statements. No one knows for sure what the future will be like. Also remember that the employment outlook is a general statement about an industry and does not necessarily apply to everyone. A determined and talented person may be able to find a job in an industry or career with the worst outlook. And a person without ambition and the proper training will find it difficult to find a job in even a booming industry or career field.

Where Can I Find More Information?

Each chapter concludes with a "For More Info" section. It lists resources that you can contact to find out more about the field and careers in the field. You will find the names, addresses, phone numbers, and websites of advertising- and marketing-oriented associations and organizations.

Extras

Every chapter has a few extras. There are photos that show advertising and marketing workers in action. There are sidebars and notes on ways to explore the field, fun facts, or lists of websites and books that might be helpful. At the end of the book you will find a glossary, an index, and a "Browse and Learn More" section. The "Browse and Learn More" section lists general advertising and marketing books and websites to explore. The glossary gives brief definitions of words that relate to education, career training, or employment that you may be unfamiliar with. The index includes all the job titles mentioned in the book.

It's not too soon to think about your future. We hope you discover several possible career choices in the advertising and marketing industries. Happy hunting!

Advertising Account Executives

What Advertising Account Executives Do

Advertising account executives track the day-to-day progress of their clients' advertising campaigns. Together with a staff commonly consisting of a creative director, an art director, a copywriter, researchers, editors, graphic artists, and production specialists, the account executive monitors client campaigns from beginning to end.

Before an advertising campaign is actually launched, advertising account executives need to do a lot of prep work. They must get to know their clients' products and services, target markets, goals, competitors, and preferred media (meaning the method—print, radio, television, Internet—that the client wants to use to reach potential customers). Together with the agency team, the account executive conducts research and holds initial meetings with clients. Then the team, coordinated by the account executive, uses this information to analyze market potential and presents recommendations to the client.

After an advertising strategy has been determined and all terms have been agreed upon, the agency's creative

> ## Top Five Advertising Slogans of the 20th Century
>
> ○ Diamonds are forever (DeBeers)
> ○ Just do it (Nike)
> ○ The pause that refreshes (Coca-Cola)
> ○ Tastes great, less filling (Miller Lite)
> ○ We try harder (Avis)
>
> Source: *Advertising Age*

EXPLORING

○ Read publications like *Advertising Age* (http://www.adage.com), *Adweek* (http://www.adweek.com), and *Brandweek* (http://www.brandweek.com) to become familiar with advertising issues, trends, successes, and failures.

○ Visit the Clio Awards website (http://www.clioawards.com). Clios are given each year in the categories of TV, print, outdoor, radio, integrated media, design, Internet, and student work. The site also has information about advertising and art schools, trade associations, and links to some of the trade magazines of the industry.

○ To gain experience, become involved with advertising or promotion activities at your school for social, sports, political, or fundraising events. If your school newspaper or yearbook has paid advertising, offer to work in ad sales.

○ Ask your teacher to arrange a presentation by an advertising account executive.

staff goes to work, developing ideas and producing various ads to present to the client. During this time, the account executive works with *media buyers* (who purchase radio and television time and publication space for advertising) to develop a schedule for the project and make sure that the costs involved are within the client's budget.

When the client approves the ad campaign, production can begin. In addition to supervising the agency team, the account executive must also write reports and draft business correspondence, follow up on all client meetings, interact with outside vendors, and ensure that all segments of the advertising campaign clearly communicate the desired message. In sum, the account executive is responsible for making sure that the client is satisfied. This may require making modifications to the campaign, revising cost estimates and events schedules, and redirecting the efforts of the creative staff.

Advertising account executives have additional duties beyond tracking and handling clients' advertising campaigns. They must work to attract new clients, stay up-to-date on current advertising trends, evaluate the effectiveness of advertising programs, and track sales figures.

Education and Training

You can prepare for a career as an advertising account executive by taking a variety of courses in high school. Basic courses in English, journalism, communication, economics, psychology, business, social science, and mathematics are important for aspiring advertising account executives.

Most advertising agencies hire college graduates whose degrees can vary widely, from English, journalism, or marketing to business administration, speech communications, or fine arts. Courses in psychology, sociology, business, economics, and art are helpful. Some positions require a graduate degree in advertising, art, or marketing. Others may call for experience in a particular field, such as health care, insurance, or retail.

Two advertising account executives review proofs for an upcoming advertising campaign. (John Henley/Corbis)

To Be a Successful Advertising Account Executive, You Should . . .

○ have a good imagination
○ be able to work under pressure
○ have strong problem-solving abilities
○ be able to manage a variety of tasks and the work of others
○ have excellent communication skills
○ be aware of trends in the industry, including new advertising techniques and mediums

FOR MORE INFO

For profiles of advertising workers, career information, and trivia games, contact
Advertising Educational Foundation
220 East 42nd Street, Suite 3300
New York, NY 10017-5806
http://www.aded.org

For more information on the advertising industry, contact
American Advertising Federation
1101 Vermont Avenue, NW, Suite 500
Washington, DC 20005-6306
Tel: 202-898-0089
Email: aaf@aaf.org
http://www.aaf.org

For information on advertising agencies, contact
American Association of Advertising Agencies
405 Lexington Avenue, 18th Floor
New York, NY 10174-1801
Tel: 212-682-2500
http://www.aaaa.org

For information on the practice, study, and teaching of marketing, contact
American Marketing Association
311 South Wacker Drive, Suite 5800
Chicago, IL 60606
Tel: 800-262-1150
Email: info@ama.org
http://www.marketingpower.com

Earnings

Advertising account executives earned median annual salaries of $60,350 in 2003, according to the U.S. Department of Labor. Salaries ranged from less than $31,660 to $134,930 or more. In smaller agencies, the salary may be much lower ($20,000 or less). In larger firms, it is often much higher (over $150,000). Advertising account executives typically receive benefits such as vacation and sick leave, health and life insurance, and a retirement plan.

Outlook

The growth of the advertising industry depends on the health of the economy. In a thriving economy, advertising budgets are large, consumers tend to respond to advertising campaigns, and new products and services that require promotion are increasingly developed. The U.S. Department of Labor predicts that employment for advertising account executives will grow faster than the average over the next several years.

Competition for top-level jobs in advertising, however, will be intense. The successful candidate will be a college graduate with a lot of creativity, strong communications skills, and extensive experience in the advertising industry. Those able to speak another language will have an edge because of the increasing supply of products and services offered in foreign markets.

Advertising and Marketing Assistants

What Advertising and Marketing Assistants Do

Advertising and marketing assistants are entry-level workers who help advertising and marketing professionals get their jobs done. They are information specialists who find the facts, data, and statistics that their employers need, leaving the employers free to pursue the larger task at hand. Advertising and marketing assistants may also help with clerical duties, such as photocopying, word processing, and answering phone or email inquiries.

Advertising and marketing agencies hire advertising and marketing assistants to help them discover consumer desires and the best ways to advertise and market products. Imagine that a small toy company is considering marketing a new toy. Assistants for the company might be assigned to help find out how much it would cost to make the toy, whether or not there is already a similar toy on the market, who might buy the toy, and who might sell the toy. This would help the marketing department decide in what ways the

Top Five Advertising Jingles of the 20th Century

- You deserve a break today (McDonald's)
- Be all that you can be (U.S. Army)
- Pepsi Cola hits the spot (Pepsi Cola)
- M'm, M'm good (Campbell's)
- See the USA in your Chevrolet (General Motors)

Source: *Advertising Age*

toy should be marketed. In advertising, assistants may be asked to provide executives with statistics and quotes so that the executives may determine whether a product is appealing to a certain portion of the population.

After receiving a research assignment, advertising and marketing assistants must first determine how to locate the desired information. Sometimes this will be as simple as making a single phone call and requesting a brochure. At other times, it may involve hours, days, or even weeks of research in libraries, archives, museums, and on the Internet. Advertising and marketing assistants must then prepare the material in a report for presentation to the person who requested it. Sometimes advertising and marketing assistants are asked to present this information verbally as well.

EXPLORING

- There are many books available that describe the techniques of basic research skills. Ask a librarian or bookstore worker to help you locate them, or better yet, begin developing your research skills by tracking down materials yourself. The Internet is also full of helpful information on all subjects. To get tips on designing research surveys and analyzing data, visit http://www.hostedsurvey.com.
- You can begin exploring this career while working on your own school assignments. Use different types of resources, such as newspapers, magazines, library catalogs, computers, the Internet, and official records and documents, to locate various types of information.
- Create your own research opportunities. If you are a member of the marching band, for instance, you could research the history of the tuba and write an article for the band newsletter.
- In your local community, volunteer or work part time at a local newspaper or magazine.

Education and Training

If you want to be an advertising and marketing assistant, you must have at least a high school education. Useful courses to take at both the high school and college levels include communications, business, economics, advertising, marketing, English, psychology, and speech. With the growing trend of advertising on the Internet, you should become familiar with computers and the Web.

Many employers require that assistants have a bachelor's degree. The most popular majors for aspiring advertising and marketing assistants are advertising, marketing, English, journalism, business, and history. Some employers prefer assistants to have a degree in library science.

Advertising assistants must have strong communication skills in order to interact successfully with managers and other workers. (Ariel Skelly/Corbis)

Earnings

According to a survey by the National Association of Colleges and Employers, advertising majors entering the job market in 2003 had average starting salaries of $29,495, while marketing majors averaged $34,038.

Self-employed advertising and marketing assistants get paid by the hour or by assignment. Depending on the experience of the assistant, the complexity of the assignment, and the location of the job, pay rates may be anywhere from $7 to $25 per hour, although $10 to $12 is the norm.

Outlook

Employment for advertising and marketing assistants is expected to grow faster than the average over the next several

To Be a Successful Advertising and Marketing Assistant, You Should . . .

- ○ have a good imagination
- ○ be able to work under pressure
- ○ have strong problem-solving abilities
- ○ be able to manage a variety of tasks and the work of others

- ○ have excellent communication skills
- ○ be aware of trends in the industry, including new advertising techniques and mediums

years. There will be many applicants for each job opening, however, so those with more experience and skill will have an advantage. Starting in a small town or at a small publication can provide workers with valuable experience to move on to larger markets such as Chicago, Los Angeles, and New York.

FOR MORE INFO

For profiles of advertising workers, career information, and trivia games, contact
Advertising Educational Foundation
220 East 42nd Street, Suite 3300
New York, NY 10017-5806
http://www.aded.org

For more information on the advertising industry, contact
American Advertising Federation
1101 Vermont Avenue, NW, Suite 500
Washington, DC 20005-6306
Tel: 202-898-0089
Email: aaf@aaf.org
http://www.aaf.org

For information on advertising agencies, contact
American Association of Advertising Agencies
405 Lexington Avenue, 18th Floor
New York, NY 10174-1801
Tel: 212-682-2500
http://www.aaaa.org

For information on the practice, study, and teaching of marketing, contact
American Marketing Association
311 South Wacker Drive, Suite 5800
Chicago, IL 60606
Tel: 800-262-1150
Email: info@ama.org
http://www.marketingpower.com

Advertising and Marketing Managers

What Advertising and Marketing Managers Do

Advertising and marketing managers plan, organize, direct, and coordinate advertising and marketing campaigns. They may oversee an entire company, a geographical territory of a company's operations, or a specific department within a company.

Advertising and marketing managers implement organizational policies and goals. This may involve developing sales or promotional materials, analyzing the department's budgetary requirements, and hiring, training, and supervising staff. Advertising and marketing managers are often responsible for long-range planning for their company or department. This involves setting goals for the organization and developing a plan to meet those goals.

Advertising managers coordinate the work of researchers, copywriters, artists, telemarketers, space buyers, time buyers, and other specialists. One type of advertising manager is the *account manager,* or *account executive,* who represents the agency to its clients.

Marketing managers work with their staff and other advertising professionals to determine how ads

Advertising and Marketing Magazines

Advertising Age
http://www.adage.com

ADWEEK
http://www.adweek.com/aw/index.jsp

Mediaweek
http://www.mediaweek.com/mediaweek/index.jsp

EXPLORING

○ Develop your managerial skills by getting involved in drama, sports, school publications, or a part-time job that requires planning, scheduling, managing other workers or volunteers, fund-raising, or budgeting.

○ Try developing your own ad campaign. Take a product you enjoy, for example, a brand of soda you drink, and try to organize a written ad campaign. Consider the type of customers that you should target and what wording and images would work best to attract this audience.

○ Volunteer or work part time at a local newspaper or magazine.

○ Ask your teacher to set up an information interview with an advertising or marketing manager.

should look, where they should be placed, and when the advertising should begin. Managers must keep staff focused on the target audience and carefully time the release of an ad.

The marketing manager must also oversee his or her department in developing a distribution plan for products. If a product is expected to sell well to a certain group, then marketing professionals must decide how to deliver to members of that group based on when and where they shop.

Along with the public relations department, marketing managers contact members of the press with the aim of getting product information out to the public.

Education and Training

If you are interested in a managerial career, you should start preparing in high school by taking college preparatory classes.

Most advertising and marketing managers have a bachelor's degree in advertising, marketing, or business administration. However, degrees in English, journalism, speech communications, economics, or the fine arts are also applicable.

Earnings

According to a survey by the National Association of Colleges and Employers, advertising majors entering the job market in 2003 had average starting salaries of $29,495, while marketing

Advertising and Marketing Glossaries

Glossary of Terms Used in Advertising and Marketing Communications
http://www.garyeverhart.com/glossary_of_advertising_terms.htm

The Marketing Manager's Plain English Internet Glossary
http://www.jaderiver.com/glossary.htm

The University of Texas at Austin: Department of Advertising
http://advertising.utexas.edu/research/terms

majors averaged $34,038. Advertising managers had median annual salaries of $60,350 in 2003, according to the U.S. Department of Labor. Marketing managers earned median salaries of $83,210 in 2003.

Outlook

Employment of advertising and marketing managers is expected to grow faster than the average over the next several

A group of advertising managers discuss the merits of a recent print advertising campaign. (David Raymer/Corbis)

years. Many job openings will be the result of managers being promoted to better positions, retiring, or leaving their positions to start their own businesses. College graduates with experience, a high level of creativity, and strong communication skills should have the best job opportunities.

FOR MORE INFO

For profiles of advertising workers, career information, and trivia games, contact
Advertising Educational Foundation
220 East 42nd Street, Suite 3300
New York, NY 10017-5806
http://www.aded.org

For more information on the advertising industry, contact
American Advertising Federation
1101 Vermont Avenue, NW, Suite 500
Washington, DC 20005-6306
Tel: 202-898-0089
Email: aaf@aaf.org
http://www.aaf.org

For information on advertising agencies, contact
American Association of Advertising Agencies
405 Lexington Avenue, 18th Floor
New York, NY 10174-1801
Tel: 212-682-2500
http://www.aaaa.org

For information on the practice, study, and teaching of marketing, contact
American Marketing Association
311 South Wacker Drive, Suite 5800
Chicago, IL 60606
Tel: 800-262-1150
Email: info@ama.org
http://www.marketingpower.com

Art Directors

What Art Directors Do

Art directors are in charge of all images that appear in print (advertisements, newspapers, magazines, and books) and on screen (television, movies, videos, and the Web). Art directors work at advertising agencies, publishing companies, film studios, theater companies, and other organizations that produce or use visual elements such as photography, illustrations, props, costumes, and sets. Art directors hire illustrators, photographers, animators, set and costume designers, and models and find existing illustrations and photos. Sometimes they combine new and existing art to create a desired visual effect.

Some art directors work with printed material, such as newspapers, magazines, and books. They are experts in arranging the text, pictures, and other visual elements, as well as using color, photography, and different kinds of lettering called typefaces.

In print media, art directors sketch a design of what the page will look like. They block out areas for text, artwork, and other graphics. The art director then selects illustrators, photographers, or graphic designers to create the finished art for the project. A production editor or graphic designer puts the finished pieces together into a final form, usually in a computer layout file. The art director oversees every part of the process and gives approval or orders changes. Once the art director is satisfied with the final proof, the project is ready to be printed.

Did You Know?

There are approximately 8,930 art directors employed in advertising and related industries, according to the U.S. Department of Labor.

EXPLORING

○ Join a free online art club, such as Paleta: The Art Project (http://www.paletaworld.org).

○ Work on the staff of your school newspaper, magazine, or yearbook.

○ Develop your own artistic talent by reading books and practicing drawing skills or taking art classes.

○ Study product packaging; advertisements in magazines, newspapers, and websites; and television commercials. Notice color, composition, balance, mood, and other visual elements.

○ Get a part-time job in the art department of a local newspaper or advertising agency.

Technology has been playing an increasingly important role in the art director's job. Most art directors, for example, use a variety of computer software programs, including Adobe InDesign, PageMaker, FrameMaker, Illustrator, and Photoshop; QuarkXPress; and CorelDRAW. Many others create and oversee websites for clients and work with other interactive media and materials, including CD-ROM, touch-screens, multidimensional visuals, and new animation programs.

Education and Training

To prepare for a career as an art director, concentrate on art and computer classes, as well as math. Most art directors have at least a bachelor's degree, usually in graphic design or fine art. If you plan to work in advertising or marketing, be sure to take college classes in these disciplines; some art directors even have degrees in these fields.

Art directors rarely start out as art directors. Their first jobs may be as graphic designers, production assistants, or illustrators. As they gain experience and learn the ins and outs of their particular industry, they move into higher positions until they become art directors.

Earnings

Art directors who are employed in advertising and related services had mean annual salaries of $73,950 in 2003, according to the U.S. Department of Labor. Salaries for art directors employed in all industries ranged from less than $34,160 to $114,390 or more.

Most companies employing art directors offer insurance benefits, a retirement plan, and other incentives and bonuses.

Outlook

There will always be a need for talented art directors to oversee the creation of advertising and marketing campaigns and materials, books and other publications, and film and television

FOR MORE INFO

For profiles of advertising workers, career information, and trivia games, contact
Advertising Educational Foundation
220 East 42nd Street, Suite 3300
New York, NY 10017-5806
http://www.aded.org

For more information on the advertising industry, contact
American Advertising Federation
1101 Vermont Avenue, NW, Suite 500
Washington, DC 20005-6306
Tel: 202-898-0089
Email: aaf@aaf.org
http://www.aaf.org

For information on advertising agencies, contact
American Association of Advertising Agencies
405 Lexington Avenue, 18th Floor
New York, NY 10174-1801

Tel: 212-682-2500
http://www.aaaa.org

For more information on graphic design, contact
American Institute of Graphic Arts
164 Fifth Avenue
New York, NY 10010
Tel: 212-807-1990
http://www.aiga.org

The Art Directors Club is an international, nonprofit organization of directors in advertising, graphic design, interactive media, broadcast design, typography, packaging, photography, illustration, and related disciplines. For information, contact
Art Directors Club
106 West 29th Street
New York, NY 10001
Tel: 212-643-1440
Email: info@adcglobal.org
http://www.adcglobal.org

To Be a Successful Art Director, You Should . . .

- ○ be creative and imaginative
- ○ have knowledge of computer hardware and software
- ○ work well with all types of people
- ○ be able to handle the stress of constant deadlines
- ○ have excellent time management skills
- ○ stay up-to-date with current technology

productions. Competition for these jobs will be stiff, though. It takes many years assisting in design and layout before you can become a director.

One area that shows particularly good promise for growth is the retail industry, since more and more large retail establishments—especially catalog houses—will be employing in-house advertising art directors.

Buyers

What Buyers Do

There are two main types of *buyers*. *Wholesale buyers* purchase merchandise directly from manufacturers and resell it to retail stores, commercial establishments such as hotels, and other institutions. *Retail buyers* purchase goods from wholesalers (and occasionally from manufacturers) for resale to the general public in retail stores. Buyers must understand their customers' needs and be able to purchase goods at an appropriate price and in sufficient quantity. Sometimes a buyer is referred to by the type of merchandise purchased— for example, jewelry buyer or toy buyer. *Government buyers* have similar responsibilities but need to be especially sensitive to concerns of fairness and ethics since they use public money to make their purchases.

Retail buyers may supervise salespeople as well as purchase goods. When a new product appears on the shelves, for example, buyers may work with salespeople to point out its distinctive features. Thus, this type of retail buyer thus takes responsibility for product marketing. Another type of retail buyer is concerned only with purchasing and has no supervisory responsibilities. These buyers cooperate with the sales staff to promote maximum sales.

Where Do Buyers Work?

According to the U.S. Department of Labor, there are 527,000 purchasing managers, buyers, and purchasing agents employed throughout the country. About 42 percent work in wholesale trade and manufacturing, 15,600 work in management, and 16,570 in farm products. Approximately 7,900 work in retail trade, such as for grocery stores and department stores. Others work in businesses that provide services and in government agencies.

EXPLORING

○ Gain retail experience through part-time or summer employment in a store.
○ Participate in door-to-door selling programs through your school or a club
○ Keep a close eye on store product displays and newspaper circulars. Develop a sense of what products sell best at certain times of the year.

All retail buyers must understand the basic policies of their stores. A retail buyer's purchases are affected by the size of the buyer's annual budget, the kind of merchandise needed in each buying season (for example, beach towels in the summer and snow shovels in the winter), and trends in the market. Buyers often work with *assistant buyers,* who spend much of their time maintaining sales and inventory records.

All buyers must be experts in the merchandise that they purchase. They often order goods months ahead of the sale date, so they must be able to predict how well the product will sell based upon cost, style, and competitive items. Buyers must also be well acquainted with the best sources from which to buy each product.

A retail buyer may place orders through traveling salespeople (ordering from samples or catalogs), order by mail or by telephone directly from the manufacturer or wholesaler, or travel to key cities to visit merchandise showrooms and manufacturing establishments. Most use a combination of these approaches.

Department stores and other large chains usually have central buying positions. *Central buyers* order products in unusually large quantities. Goods purchased by central buyers may be marketed under the manufacturer's label (as is normally done) or ordered with the store's label or a chain brand name.

Independent stores often work with *resident buyers,* who purchase merchandise for a large number of stores. By purchasing large quantities of the same product, resident buyers can obtain the same types of discounts enjoyed by large chain stores and then pass along the savings to their customers.

Education and Training

A high school diploma generally is required for entering the field of buying. Useful high school courses include mathematics, business, English, and economics.

A college degree may not be a requirement for becoming a buyer, but it is becoming increasingly important, especially for advancement. Many buyers have bachelor's degrees in business, engineering, or economics. Some colleges and universities also offer majors in purchasing or materials management. Regardless of the major, useful courses in preparation for a career in buying include accounting, economics, commercial law, finance, marketing, and various business classes, such as business communications, business organization and management, and computer applications in business.

Earnings

The U.S. Department of Labor reports the median annual income for wholesale and retail buyers was $42,170 in 2003. Most buyers made between $24,350 and $80,690 annually. Buyers' salaries vary widely depending on their responsibilities, place of employment, and number of years in the field.

Most buyers receive the usual benefits, such as vacation, sick leave, life and health insurance, and pension plans. Retail buyers may receive cash bonuses for their work and may also

To Be a Buyer, You Should . . .

- be organized
- have excellent decision-making skills
- have a good sense of shoppers' tastes
- have excellent leadership and people skills
- develop a strong list of retail and wholesale contacts

FOR MORE INFO

For career information and job listings, contact
American Purchasing Society
8 East Galena Boulevard, Suite 203
Aurora, IL 60506
Tel: 630-859-0250
http://www.american-purchasing.com

For information on the magazine Your Future Purchasing Career, *lists of colleges with purchasing programs, and interviews with people in the field, contact the ISM.*
Institute for Supply Management (ISM)
PO Box 22160
Tempe, AZ 85285-2160
Tel: 800-888-6276
http://www.ism.ws

For information on purchasing careers in the government and certification, contact
National Institute of Government Purchasing
151 Spring Street
Herndon, VA 20170-5223
Tel: 800-367-6447
http://www.nigp.org

For materials on educational programs in the retail industry, contact
National Retail Federation
325 7th Street, NW, Suite 1100
Washington, DC 20004
Tel: 800-673-4692
http://www.nrf.com

receive discounts on merchandise they purchase from their employer.

Outlook

According to the U.S. Department of Labor, employment of wholesale and retail buyers is projected to grow slower than the average through 2012. The large number of business mergers and acquisitions will result in the blending of buying departments and the elimination of some jobs. In addition, the increased use of computers for buying functions will result in fewer new jobs for buyers. Some job openings will result from the need to hire replacement workers for those who leave the field. On the other hand, companies in the service sector are beginning to realize the advantages of having professional buyers.

Composers

What Composers Do

Composers, often known as *jingle writers* in the advertising industry, create the music (and sometimes lyrics) heard on television and radio commercials. This combination of music and lyrics is called a jingle. To advertise a product or service, a jingle may feature voice and background music that alternate or a song that contains words (provided by the client and/or the composer) that conveys all the necessary information.

Composers are employed by advertising agencies, music production houses, and recording studios. Other composers write music for musical stage shows, movies, ballet and opera companies, orchestras, pop and rock bands, jazz combos, and other musical performing groups.

To create a jingle, composers meet with clients to discuss the advertising jingle's theme, length, style, the number and types of performers, and project deadline. They are usually told whether the jingle should feature music only, lyrics only, or both music and lyrics. If lyrics are to be used, composers may be given catch phrases that need to be worked into the jingle. Some composers may be given only a little information about a product or service to be advertised and asked to use their creativity to create a jingle that effectively sells the product or service.

To create a jingle, composers use their music training and their own

A Good Advertising Jingle . . .

- ○ is catchy and memorable
- ○ effectively sells a product or service
- ○ is often repetitive in order to reinforce its main theme
- ○ doesn't contain too many ideas or clunky strings of words

EXPLORING

- Read the *Songwriter's Market* (Cincinnati: Writers Digest Books, 2003) to learn more about potential employers.
- Read books about music and composers and their careers.
- Attend concerts and recitals.
- Listen to advertising jingles and related compositions. Write down what you like or dislike about each selection.
- Learn to play a musical instrument, such as the piano, keyboard, guitar, violin, or cello.
- Create an advertising jingle for one of your favorite products.
- Participate in musical programs offered by local schools, YMCA/ YWCAs, and community centers.
- Form or join a musical group and try to write music for your group to perform.

personal sense of melody, harmony, rhythm, and structure. Some compose music as they play an instrument and may or may not write it down. When they complete a rough version of the jingle, they submit it to their client for review. After the piece is reviewed and revisions (such as fewer words, peppier music, more serious music, and so forth) are suggested, the composer makes the required changes and creates the final version of the jingle. The composer usually attends rehearsals and works with performers to create the jingle. Once finished, the composer may still have to further revise the jingle until the client is satisfied.

Composers work at home, in advertising offices, or in music studios. Some need to work alone to plan and build their musical ideas and others work with fellow musicians. Composing can take many long hours of work, and composing jobs may be irregular. However, it is extremely satisfying for composers to hear their music performed, and successful composers, especially in the advertising industry, can earn a lot of money.

In addition to creating advertising jingles, freelance composers perform other tasks to support their businesses. They prepare invoices for services rendered, market their business to potential new clients by sending out demo tapes, and stay up to date with music technology—which changes quickly.

Words to Learn

Composers use these words to tell musicians how loud or soft to play:

Pianissimo (pp) very soft

Piano (p) soft

Mezzopiano (mp) half-soft

Diminuendo or Descrescendo (dim; decresc. or >) growing softer

Mezzoforte (mf) half loud

Forte (f) loud

Fortissimo (ff) very loud

Crescendo (cres. or <) growing louder

Fortepiano (fp) loud, then soft

Sforzando or sforzato (sf; sfz) sudden, strong accent

Education and Training

There is no specific course of training that will help you to become a composer. Many composers begin composing from a very early age and receive tutoring and training to encourage their talent. Musically inclined students should continue their private studies and take advantage of everything musical their high school offers. Studying music helps you develop and express your musical ideas.

All composers need to have a good ear and be able to notate, or write down, their music.

Earnings

The U.S. Department of Labor reports that salaried composers had earnings that ranged from less than $14,870 to $72,710 or more in 2003. Median earnings for composers were $32,530 in 2003.

Outlook

Employment for composers will grow about as fast as the average over the next several years. As long as there are commercials, movies, musicals, operas, and orchestras, and other musical performances, there will be a need
for composers to write music.

FOR MORE INFO

*For professional and artistic development
resources, contact*
American Composers Forum
332 Minnesota Street, Suite East 145
St. Paul, MN 55101-1300
Tel: 651-228-1407
Email: mail@composersforum.org
http://www.composersforum.org

For career information, contact
**American Federation of
Musicians of the United States
and Canada**
1501 Broadway, Suite 600
New York, NY 10036
Tel: 212-869-1330
Email: info@afm.org
http://www.afm.org

*For articles on songwriting, information on
workshops and awards, and practical infor-
mation about the business of music, contact*
**American Society of Composers,
Authors, and Publishers**
One Lincoln Plaza
New York, NY 10023
Tel: 800-952-7227

Email: info@ascap.com
http://www.ascap.com

*This organization represents songwriters,
composers, and music publishers. Its website
has useful information on the industry.*
Broadcast Music Inc.
320 West 57th Street
New York, NY 10019-3790
Tel: 212-586-2000
http://www.bmi.com

*The Meet the Composer website has informa-
tion on awards and residencies as well as
interviews with composers active in the field
today.*
Meet the Composer
75 Ninth Avenue, 3R Suite C
New York, NY 10011
Tel: 212-645-6949
http://www.meetthecomposer.org

For information on competitions, contact
Society of Composers
Old Chelsea State
Box 450
New York, NY 10113-0450
http://www.societyofcomposers.org

Copywriters

What Copywriters Do

Copywriters' main goal is to persuade the general public to choose or favor certain goods, services, and personalities. Copywriters and their assistants write the words of advertisements, including the written text in print ads and the spoken words in radio and television ads, which are also called spots.

Copywriters may have to come up with their own idea and words for an ad, but generally the client's account manger and head designer generate the idea. Once the idea behind the ad is presented, copywriters begin gathering as much information as possible about the client through library research, interviews, observation, and other methods. They study advertising trends and review surveys of consumer preferences. They keep extensive notes from which they will draw material for the ad. Once their research has been organized, copywriters begin working on the written components of the ad. They may have a standard theme or pitch to work with that has been developed in previous ads. One such example, using what is called a tagline, is seen in the popular milk campaign, "Milk: It does a body good." This campaign promotes milk's health benefits and other advantages—beauty, athleticism, and intelligence.

The process of developing copy is exciting, although it can also involve

Did You Know?

- There are approximately 21,000 advertising firms nationwide, employing over 300,000 workers.
- Copywriters and editors hold approximately 10,000 jobs in the industry.
- The advertising industry will grow by 19 percent over the next decade.

Source: U.S. Department of Labor

EXPLORING

○ Read and listen to all sorts of advertisements. This will expose you to both good and bad writing styles and techniques and help you to identify why one approach works better than another.

○ Test your interest and aptitude in the field of writing by working as a reporter or writer on your school newspaper, yearbook, and literary magazine.

○ Take writing courses and workshops offered by your school or your local community to sharpen your writing skills.

○ Tour local advertising firms, newspapers, publishers, or radio and television stations and interview some of the writers who work there.

detailed and solitary work. After researching one idea, a writer might discover that a different perspective or related topic would be more effective, entertaining, or marketable.

When working on assignment, copywriters submit their ad drafts to their editor or the advertising account executive for approval. Writers often work through several drafts. They write and rewrite sections of the material as they proceed, searching for just the right way to promote the product, service, or other client need.

Copywriters may also write articles, bulletins, news releases, sales letters, speeches, and other related informative and promotional material. In addition to working in advertising, some copywriters work for public relations firms or in communications departments of large companies.

Education and Training

If you are interested in becoming a copywriter, take high school courses in English, literature, foreign languages, business, computer science, and typing. Work on your school newspaper, yearbook, or literary magazine to gain writing experience.

You must earn a college degree to be eligible for most copywriting positions. Many employers prefer that you have a broad liberal arts background or a major in English, literature, history, philosophy, or one of the social sciences. Other employers want employees who have had communications or journalism training in college. A number of schools offer courses in copywriting and other business writing.

Earnings

The U.S. Department of Labor reports that writers (including copywriters) who were employed in advertising and related services had mean annual earnings of $70,740 in 2003. Salaries for all writers ranged from less than $22,090 to $87,390 or more annually.

Outlook

The outlook for the advertising industry as a whole looks promising. One important trend that will affect the employment of copywriters is specialization. Expected high-growth areas include foreign-language programming, advertising aimed at specific ethnic groups, advertising targeted at the over-50 market, special events advertising and marketing, and direct marketing campaigns for retailers and technological companies. Copywriters who can offer skills such as the ability

To Be a Successful Copywriter, You Should . . .

- be creative and able to express ideas clearly
- have strong communication skills—both written and oral
- be a skilled researcher
- be computer literate
- be curious, persistent, and resourceful
- have the ability to work under pressure and tight deadlines

FOR MORE INFO

For profiles of advertising workers, career information, and trivia games, contact
Advertising Educational Foundation
220 East 42nd Street, Suite 3300
New York, NY 10017-5806
http://www.aded.org

For more information on the advertising industry, contact
American Advertising Federation
1101 Vermont Avenue, NW, Suite 500
Washington, DC 20005-6306
Tel: 202-898-0089
Email: aaf@aaf.org
http://www.aaf.org

For information on advertising agencies, contact
American Association of Advertising Agencies
405 Lexington Avenue, 18th Floor
New York, NY 10174-1801
Tel: 212-682-2500
http://www.aaaa.org

For information about working as a writer and union membership, contact
National Writers Union
113 University Place, 6th Floor
New York, NY 10003
Tel: 212-254-0279
Email: nwu@nwu.org
http://www.nwu.org

to speak a foreign language will be in demand.

In addition, the explosion of online advertising has created a wealth of jobs, and companies are responding by placing advertising on the Web and creating websites that allow customers the ease and convenience of online shopping. From flowers to antiques, clothing to furniture, virtually everything can be purchased online. All of the goods and services available online require copywriters to write ads that will promote and sell. Individuals with extensive computer skills will be at an advantage as a result.

People entering this field should realize that the competition for jobs is extremely keen. The appeal of writing and advertising jobs will continue to grow, as many young graduates find the industry glamorous and exciting.

Demographers

What Demographers Do

Demographers collect and study facts about society's population—births, marriages, deaths, education, and income levels. Their population studies tell what the society is really like and help experts predict economic and social trends.

Demographers use computers to gather and analyze the millions of pieces of information they need to make their forecasts. It is up to the individual demographer to know how to read the statistics and put them together in a meaningful way.

Demographers work for both private companies and government agencies. Private companies need demographers' collections of facts, or statistics, to help them improve their products or services and know who will buy them. For example, a retail chain might use a demographer's study to help decide the best location to open a new store. Other demographers may help an advertising and marketing firm study the demographics of car buyers in a community for its client. The company will use this information to help its client (a local car dealership) formulate a marketing campaign. For example, if the demographic study revealed that many young families lived in the community, the dealership might focus on selling minivans and

Demography- and Statistics-Oriented Websites

CIA World Fact Book
http://www.odci.gov/cia/publications/factbook

FedStats
http://www.fedstats.gov

The Gallup Organization
http://www.gallup.com

HarrisInteractive
http://www.harrisinteractive.com

U.S. Bureau of the Census
http://www.census.gov

Why Do We Need Population Statistics?

Population statistics, the basic tool of demography, include total population figures, population density (the average number of persons inhabiting each square mile), age, sex, and racial groupings, among other data.

Accurate population statistics are necessary in planning advertising and marketing campaigns, immigration policies, and public health programs, as well as the basis for assigning seats in the House of Representatives among the states.

SUVs to these families. If the demographic study revealed that the community consisted of mostly young people only a few years out of college, the dealership might instead try to sell sportier and/or more economical cars to these potential buyers.

Local, state, and federal government agencies use demographers to help them provide enough of the right kinds of transportation, education, police, and health services. Demographers may also teach in colleges and universities or work as consultants for private companies or communities as a whole.

Education and Training

Students interested in this field should be good at solving logic problems and have strong skills in numbers and mathematics, especially algebra and geometry. In high school, you should take classes in social

EXPLORING

○ Conduct your own demographic survey of an organization or group, such as your school or after-school club.

○ Talk with demographers employed in the advertising or marketing industries about the pros and cons of the career.

○ If you are in high school, get a part-time or summer job at a company with a statistical research department. This will give you insight into the career of demographer.

studies, English, and mathematics. Training in computer science also is helpful.

Demographers need a college degree in sociology or public health with special studies in demography. If you are interested in specializing in advertising or marketing, you might want to minor in one of these disciplines. Many entry-level jobs require a master's degree.

As the field gets more competitive, many demographers (especially those who wish to work for the federal government) will earn a doctorate in sociology. The most successful demographers specialize in one area. You must also keep up with advances in the field by continuing your education throughout your career.

FOR MORE INFO

For profiles of advertising workers, career information, and trivia games, contact
Advertising Educational Foundation
220 East 42nd Street, Suite 3300
New York, NY 10017-5806
http://www.aded.org

For information on practicing, studying, and teaching marketing, contact
American Marketing Association
311 South Wacker Drive, Suite 5800
Chicago, IL 60606
Tel: 800-262-1150
Email: info@ama.org
http://www.marketingpower.com

For free career publications and a list of accredited schools, contact
American Sociological Association
1307 New York Avenue, NW, Suite 700
Washington, DC 20005

Tel: 202-383-9005
Email: executive.office@asanet.org
http://www.asanet.org

For information on careers and accredited schools, contact
Population Association of America
8630 Fenton Street, Suite 722
Silver Spring, MD 20910-3812
Tel: 301-565-6710
Email: info@popassoc.org
http://www.popassoc.org

For information about the U.S. Census Bureau, contact
U.S. Census Bureau
Public Information Office
U.S. Census Bureau
4700 Silver Hill Road
Washington, DC 20233-0001
http://www.census.gov

Earnings

Earnings vary according to demographers' education, training, and place of employment. Social scientists (including sociologists who specialize in demography) with a bachelor's degree in sociology received average starting salaries of $28,065 in 2003, according to the National Association of Colleges and Employers. Salaries range from $22,000 to $70,000 annually.

Outlook

There is a large amount of fact-gathering and social science research going on in the United States. As a result, employment of demographers will grow about as fast as the average over the next several years. Job opportunities will be greatest in and around large cities, because that is where many advertising and marketing agencies are located.

Fashion Coordinators

What Fashion Coordinators Do

Fashion coordinators are responsible for promoting fashion trends through shows and other promotional events for clothing companies and designers. Some are responsible for a particular department, for example, men's apparel, while others may be responsible for the promotion of the entire apparel and accessories line. Most fashion coordinators work for design firms, retail corporations, and apparel centers. Some work in the entertainment industry.

Every show sends a particular message, or theme, to the audience. For example, what will be important in fashion for the next season? Leather? Wool? Fur? It is the fashion coordinator's job to convey the designer's message through a show's fashions, lighting, backdrop, music, models, and commentary.

There are different types of fashion shows. Vendor or designer shows arrive at the coordinator's office almost pre-packaged. The outfits are already accessorized and are boxed in the order in which the clothes should be shown. The designer is also in charge of the commentary and backdrops. Vendor shows typically take only a few days to produce. The designer or design firm owns the rights to these fashion shows. Many vendor-type fashion shows take place within the department's sales floor so the public can shop for the clothes as soon as the show ends.

Trend shows are owned by the retailer and are produced by the fashion

---

To Become a Fashion Coordinator, You Should . . .

- be hard-working and organized
- be able to juggle many tasks simultaneously
- have a good eye for color, design, and what is fashionable
- remain up-to-date on current trends in fashion, music, and culture

EXPLORING

○ Volunteer at fashion shows or simply attend one to see all of the elements involved.

○ Read fashion magazines and keep up on what's popular from year to year.

○ Volunteer to produce a fashion show in your school or community group. Your models can be fellow classmates; clothing and accessories can be borrowed from the local stores who might want to support the project. Adopt a theme that would interest your peers, say, fashions for the prom or the latest in summer swimwear.

○ Put together a calendar featuring a particular high school group. Pick a theme that is interesting and challenging, such as spotlighting an athletic team, drama club members, or even favorite teachers.

coordinator and his or her staff. With these shows, coordinators are responsible for putting together outfits and accessories, choosing the choreography and staging, and most importantly, deciding on the message. Trend shows are usually produced two or three times a year and scheduled to coincide with the upcoming fashion season. It often takes a few weeks or a month to put together a trend show.

There are several steps to producing a show. First, a budget is set. Then models must be cast to fit the type of clothes. Sometimes as many as 300 models audition before the coordinator selects the final 30 or so to work the trend show. Coordinators often use trusted *modeling agents* to find the best men, women, or children. *Stylists* are used to give the models and their clothes a finished look. *Hairdressers, makeup artists,* and *dressers* prepare the models before the show and during outfit changes. *Production workers* are responsible for finding the right music and lighting. The fashion coordinator and assistants are also responsible for the promotion and execution of a fashion show. They send invitations to the public and media and prepare advertising, as well as set up chairs and props and check on other last minute details.

Fashion coordinators often travel to meet with designers, many of whom are headquartered in New York. Another important part of a fashion coordinator's job is to help with promotion of a store's fashion lines through television or newspaper and magazine spreads.

The fashion coordinator's office is part of the marketing side of the fashion industry. Coordinators work alongside *trend forecasters, product developers,* and *planners* in promoting current fashion trends, as well as predicting what the public will desire in fashion for the future.

Education

If your high school does not offer specialized fashion courses, you can still prepare for this work by taking classes such as family and consumer science, art, English, and speech.

Although not required, a bachelor's degree plus experience will give you an edge over the candidate working solely on past job skills. Most fashion coordinators have degrees in fashion design and merchandising, marketing, or other business-related courses. Most fashion coordinators also complete an internship before graduating.

Earnings

According to industry experts, most salaried stylists should expect to earn from $25,000 to $37,000 annually. Stylists working on a freelance basis can also earn as much, though they are paid only after a project is completed as opposed to weekly or bimonthly. Some successful fashion coordinators,

Moving Up

The fashion coordinator position is considered a high rung in the fashion industry ladder. One advancement possibility for a fashion coordinator would be to move deeper into the marketing side of the fashion industry by working as a product developer or fashion forecaster. *Product developers* produce in-house lines of apparel and accessories. *Fashion forecasters,* using a variety of tools, such as surveys, current styles, and market research, try to predict future trends in fashion.

Another way to advance in this career is by transferring to a larger company or design firm, which usually means more responsibilities and a higher salary.

especially those employed by larger corporations or well-known design houses, can earn over $100,000 a year.

Outlook

Employment for fashion coordinators should be good in coming years. Many opportunities will occur as a result of the creation of new positions in the field or current employees retiring or leaving the workforce for other reasons. Most jobs in the United States will be available in densely populated areas, especially New York City, Chicago, Los Angeles, and Miami.

FOR MORE INFO

For information on the industry, student membership, or networking opportunities, contact
Fashion Group International Inc.
8 West 40th Street, 7th Floor
New York, NY 10018
Tel: 212-302-5511
Email: info@fgi.org
http://www.fgi.org

To learn more about the programs and exhibitions offered at FIT, check out their website or contact
Fashion Institute of Technology (FIT)
Seventh Avenue at 27th Street
New York, NY 10001-5992
Tel: 212-217-7999
Email: FITinfo@fitsuny.edu
http://www.fitnyc.suny.edu

One of the degrees offered at this school is in fashion marketing and management. For
information on admissions and to view sample student portfolios, check out the website.
Illinois Institute of Art at Chicago
350 North Orleans Street, #136
Chicago, IL 60654
Tel: 800-351-3450
http://www.ilia.aii.edu

7th on Sixth offers venues for designers to showcase their latest fashions. For volunteer opportunities, contact
7th on Sixth
IMG
22 East 71st Street
New York, NY 10021
Tel: 212-253-2692
Email: info@7thonsixth.com
http://www.7thonsixth.com

For subscription information, contact
Women's Wear Daily
http://www.wwd.com

Fashion Illustrators and Photographers

What Fashion Illustrators and Photographers Do

Fashion illustrators and photographers work in a glamorous but intense environment. Fashion illustrators create illustrations that appear in print and electronic formats. Illustrations are used to advertise new fashions, promote models, and popularize certain designers. Some illustrators provide artwork to accompany editorial pieces in fashion magazines. Catalog companies also employ illustrators to provide the artwork for print or online publications.

Fashion illustrators work with fashion designers, editors, and models. They make sketches from designers' notes or they may sketch live models during runway shows or other fashion presentations. They use pencils, pen and ink, charcoal, paint, airbrush, or a combination of media to create their work. In addition to working with pens and paper, fashion illustrators also need to be able to work with computer programs designed to manipulate their artwork.

The advertising industry is probably the largest employer of fashion photographers. These artists create the

Early Fashion Illustration?

Illustration featured prominently in the ancient civilizations of Mesopotamia, Egypt, and later Greek and Roman civilizations. Drawings of figures conveying power or ideas have also been found among ancient Assyrian, Babylonian, Egyptian, and Chinese societies. Modern illustration began during the Renaissance of the 15th and 16th centuries, with the work of Leonardo da Vinci, Andreas Vesalius, and Michelangelo Buonarotti.

A fashion photographer prepares for a shoot in her home studio. (Ariel Skelley/Corbis)

pictures that sell clothing, cosmetics, shoes, accessories, and beauty products. Fashion photographers' tools include cameras, film, filters, lenses, tripods, and lighting equipment. Fashion photographers sometimes are in charge of choosing a location for a shoot, such as a beach or a train station, or they may construct a studio set. They work with a team of people, including designers, editors, models, photo stylists, hair stylists, and makeup artists. Catalog shots tend to be straightforward, showing as much detail of the clothing as possible. Photographs for fashion magazines and advertising are often more creative, conveying a particular mood and emphasizing glamour.

The fashion world is fast paced and competitive. The hours can be long, and there is pressure to produce good work under tight deadlines. Illustrators and photographers may have to face rejection of their work when they are starting out until they can earn a reputation and develop a style that is in demand.

Education and Training

There are no formal education requirements for fashion illustrators or photographers. For both photographers and illustrators, the best education is practice. As you continue to practice your art, you will begin to build a portfolio of your work, or a collection of the best of your sketches or photos. There are some vocational, fashion, and art schools that offer classes in fashion illustration. These classes not only teach you art technique but also teach you how to assemble and present your portfolio. Pho-

Try It Yourself

The best way to see if you have what it takes to become a fashion illustrator is to start drawing. Use the following website to practice drawing basic modeling figures and read tips about using other materials such as glue, pens, and mounting boards.

Fashion Drawing Tutorial Tips
http://www.fashion-era.com/drawing_fashion.htm

tography programs are widely available from the associate's degree level to the bachelor's degree level. Photographers can also apply to be apprentices to established photographers.

Earnings

The U.S. Department of Labor reports that salaried fine artists, including illustrators, had earnings that ranged from less than $17,160 to $74,080 or more in 2003. Illustrators employed in advertising and related services had average annual incomes of $51,560. Photographers employed in all industries had median annual earnings of $25,050 in 2003. Salaries ranged from less than $14,610 to $51,960 or more annually.

Outlook

Employment for visual artists and photographers is expected to grow as fast as the average over the next several years. For illustrators and photographers specifically working in fashion,

EXPLORING

○ Take drawing and photography classes offered by your school or a community center.
○ Join your school's yearbook, newspaper, or literary magazine. These publications often include student illustrations and photographs along with text.
○ Apply for a part-time job at an art supply, photography, or retail clothing store.
○ Explore your interest in the fashion field by reading fashion magazines that will keep you up-to-date on fashion trends and styles in advertising, photography, and art.

employment will likely depend on the economic health of advertising firms, magazines, newspapers, and fashion houses and other businesses involved in fashion. The outlook for these businesses currently looks strong.

FOR MORE INFO

For information on college programs in fashion design, advertising, and design, contact
International Academy of Design and Technology-Chicago
One North State Street, Suite 400
Chicago, IL 60602-3300
http://www.iadtchicago.com

International Academy of Design and Technology-Orlando
5959 Lake Ellenor Drive
Orlando, FL 32809
http://www.iadt.edu

This organization provides training, publishes its own magazine, and offers various services for its members.
Professional Photographers of America
229 Peachtree Street, NE, Suite 2200
Atlanta, GA 30303
Tel: 800-786-6277
Email: csc@ppa.com
http://www.ppa.com

This national institution promotes and stimulates interest in the art of illustration by offering exhibits, lectures, educational programs, and social interchange.
Society of Illustrators
128 East 63rd Street
New York, NY 10021-7303
Tel: 212-838-2560
http://www.societyillustrators.org

This website allows you to browse through galleries of hundreds of established fashion photographers.
FashionBook.com
http://www.fashionbook.com

Visit this site for more career advice.
Fashion Net: How to Become a Fashion Photographer
http://www.fashion.net/howto/photography

Visit this site to view several examples of fashion sketches.
Metrofashion
http://www.metrofashion.com/sketches.html

Graphic Designers

What Graphic Designers Do

Graphic designers design a wide variety of materials including advertisements, displays, packaging, signs, computer graphics and games, book and magazine covers and interiors, animated characters, websites, and company logos to fit the needs and preferences of their various clients.

Graphic designers receive materials for their assignments from advertising and marketing managers, editors and writers, illustrators, and photographers. They might receive special instructions from art directors or publishers. They have to consider the medium—print, computer, or film—and the audience. They decide on a central point of focus, such as the type of magazine in which an advertisement might appear or the name of a product on a package. They size the lettering; choose and size the artwork, whether it's an illustration, photograph, or logo; and choose colors. Some graphic designers create logos for companies or draw charts and graphs.

Graphic design is a process. For example, when designing an advertisement that will appear in a magazine, designers make two or three rough designs for the client to look at. The client might choose one of the designs immediately, or ask a designer to change the type size, color, or another element. Designers rework their pieces until their clients are satisfied. Then they prepare the final design.

Type Choices

lower case	SMALL CAPS
UPPER CASE	underline
roman	shadow
bold	outline
italic	serif
bold italic	san serif

EXPLORING

○ Take as many art and design courses as you can. If your school does not offer them, you might be able to find them offered at community centers or art schools.

○ Learn different software programs for page layout and illustration.

○ Participate in school and community projects that call for design talents. These might include building sets for plays, setting up exhibits, planning seasonal and holiday displays, and preparing concert programs and other printed materials.

○ Work on the layout of your school newspaper or yearbook.

Each medium is different. In product packaging, designers must be able to visualize a three-dimensional object that will be printed from a flat piece of artwork. Websites require a different arrangement of type and pictures than magazine pages. Other graphic designers work in film and television, designing the credits and other type that appears on screen. Others work on animated graphics, maps, and charts. Graphic designers usually specialize in one of these media.

Graphic designers are employed by advertising and marketing firms, publishing companies, printers, design studios, television studios, manufacturing firms, and retail stores. Many designers work independently as freelancers. All designers today do their work on computers, using illustration, photo manipulation, scanning, and page-layout software.

Education and Training

High school classes in mathematics, art, and computer science are a good foundation for this field. Most employers prefer to hire people who have had formal art education. The best preparation after high school is a four-year art school program that leads to a bachelor of fine arts degree. There are art schools that offer a specialty in graphic design or advertising design. Some graphic designers receive their training at vocational schools that teach the required technical skills for a beginning job. Since computer skills are increasingly important, some formal education in computer graphics is highly recommended.

Designers often start out as production artists or computer graphic technicians. Some even work as art teachers before becoming full-time designers.

Earnings

Graphic designers earned salaries that ranged from less than $21,600 to $65,060 or more in 2003, according to the U.S. Department of Labor. Graphic designers employed in advertising and related industries had average annual earnings of $44,330 in 2003. Salaried designers who advance to the position of design manager or design director earn approximately $60,000 a year. The owner of a consulting firm can make $85,000 or more.

Graphic designers who work full time for advertising firms and other companies receive full benefits, including health

How Freelancers Find Clients

Many graphic designers work as freelancers. Finding clients can be difficult, especially when a designer is just starting out. Freelancers have to spend a lot of time marketing their talents and finding assignments. Here are some methods they use.

○ Friends may have contacts in different businesses. They might be able to arrange an interview with a potential client.

○ Professional organizations hold meetings and advertise available jobs for their members.

○ Demonstrations and classes can offer opportunities to meet other designers and clients.

○ Freelancers sometimes design and print a brochure that demonstrates their talent and then send it to potential clients.

○ Freelancers can also make contacts by attending meetings, lectures, or gatherings for causes that interest them. For example, a graphic designer might attend a food-related convention and meet a restaurant owner who needs menu designs or needs someone to design a newspaper advertisement.

FOR MORE INFO

For more information about careers in graphic design and a list of college programs, visit the AIGA website.

American Institute of Graphic Arts (AIGA)
164 Fifth Avenue
New York, NY 10010
Tel: 212-807-1990
Email: comments@aiga.org
http://www.aiga.org

For a list of acccredited college art and design programs, contact

National Association of Schools of Art and Design
11250 Roger Bacon Drive, Suite 21
Reston, VA 20190-5248
Tel: 703-437-0700
Email: info@arts-accredit.org
http://nasad.arts-accredit.org

For information about publication design, contact

Society of Publication Designers
60 East 42nd Street, Suite 721
New York, NY 10165
Tel: 212-983-8585
Email: mail@spd.org
http://www.spd.org

insurance, paid vacation, and sick leave. Freelance designers must pay their own insurance costs and taxes and are not compensated for vacation or sick days.

Outlook

Graphic designers should have very good employment prospects over the next several years. As computer graphic and Web-based technology continues to advance, there will be a need for well-trained graphic designers. Companies for which graphic design was once too time-consuming or costly are now sprucing up company newsletters and magazines, among other things, requiring the skills of design professionals. Competition for jobs in graphic design is expected to be strong. Beginners and designers with only average talent or without formal education and skills may have some difficulty finding jobs.

Illustrators

What Illustrators Do

Illustrators create artwork with a variety of media—pencil, pen and ink, pastels, paints (oil, acrylic, watercolor), airbrush, collage, and computer programs. Illustrations are used to decorate, describe, inform, instruct, and draw attention. Illustrations appear in magazines, newspapers, signs and billboards, packaging (everything from milk cartons to DVDs), books, websites, computer programs, greeting cards, calendars, stationery, and direct mail.

Illustrators often work as part of a creative team which includes art directors, graphic designers, photographers, and calligraphers (those who draw lettering). Most illustrators are self-employed, but some work in advertising agencies, design firms, commercial art firms, or printing and publishing companies. They are also employed in the motion picture and television industries, retail stores, catalog companies, and public relations firms.

Profile: Maxfield Parrish (1870–1966)

Maxfield Parrish was an American illustrator and painter known for his use of color and his decorative, humorous pictures.

Parrish illustrated Eugene Field's *Poems of Childhood,* Kenneth Grahame's *Golden Age,* and other books. He did advertisements, illustrations, and covers for such magazines as *Harper's Weekly.* Among his murals are Pied Piper in the Sheraton-Palace Hotel in San Francisco and Old King Cole in the St. Regis Hotel in New York City.

Parrish was born in Philadelphia and attended Haverford College and the Pennsylvania Academy of Fine Arts. He also studied with the illustrator Howard Pyle.

EXPLORING

○ Take art classes that allow you to experiment with different media.
○ Keep a sketch diary in which you draw every day.
○ Submit artwork to your school newspaper, yearbook, or literary publication.
○ Join an art club at your school or community center.
○ Make posters for school and community events.
○ View illustrations in newspapers, magazines, and books to learn more about styles and techniques.

Some illustrators specialize. *Fashion illustrators* work for advertising agencies, newspapers, catalog houses, and fashion magazines. They attend fashion shows and work closely with fashion designers to make sure clothing colors and styles are represented accurately.

Medical illustrators make drawings, paintings, and three-dimensional models of medical procedures and specimens. Their work appears in textbooks, advertisements, medical journals, videotapes, and films.

Natural science illustrators create illustrations of plants and wildlife. They often work at museums, such as the Smithsonian Institution.

Most illustrators become known for their particular style and medium (paint, pen and ink, pastel, pencil, and collage to name a few). Until they become well known, they spend a great deal of time showing their portfolio to clients.

Education and Training

To become an illustrator, you must develop your artistic and creative abilities. In high school, take art classes and learn computer illustration programs.

Talent is perhaps more important to an illustrator's success than education or training. Education, however, will teach you about new techniques and media and help you build your portfolio. Whether you plan to look for full-time employment or freelance assignments, you will need a portfolio that contains samples of your best work. Employers are especially interested in work that has been published or printed. To find a salaried position as an illustrator, you will need at least a high school diploma and preferably an associate's degree in commercial art or fine art. Most medical illustrators have master's degrees from graduate programs in medical illustration.

Licensing and certification are not required for most illustration careers. The exception is medical illustration, in which voluntary certification is available.

Earnings

The pay for illustrations can be as little as a byline (a line under the title that gives your name). In the beginning of your career a byline may be worthwhile so that many people can become familiar with your work. Experienced illustrators can earn several thousand dollars for a single work. Average earnings for full-time fine artists (including illustrators) ranged from less than $17,160 to $74,080 or more a year in 2003, according to the U.S. Department of Labor. Fine artists employed in advertising and related services had mean annual salaries of $51,560 in 2003.

Salaried illustrators generally receive good benefits, including health and life insurance, pension plans, and vacation, sick,

Learn More about It

Edwards, Betty. *The New Drawing on the Right Side of the Brain.* New York: J. P. Tarcher, 1999.

Fleishman, Michael. *Starting Your Career as a Freelance Illustrator or Graphic Designer.* New York: Watson-Guptill Publications, 2001.

Hammond, Lee. *Draw Fashion Models!* Discover Drawing Series. Cincinnati, Ohio: North Light Books, 1998.

Hodges, Elaine R. S., ed. *The Guild Handbook of Scientific Illustration.* 2nd ed. Hoboken, N.J.: John Wiley & Sons, 2003.

Ireland, Patrick John. *Figure Templates for Fashion Illustration: Over 150 Templates for Fashion Design.* London: Batsford, 2003.

FOR MORE INFO

For information on educational and career opportunities for medical illustrators, contact
Association of Medical Illustrators
6660 Del Monico Drive, Suite D-107
Colorado Springs, CO 80919-1856
Tel: 719-598-8622
Email: hq@ami.org
http://medical-illustrators.org

For information in union membership and links to portfolios of illustrators, visit the GAG website.
Graphic Artists Guild (GAG)
90 Johns Street, Suite 403
New York, NY 10038-3202
Tel: 212-791-3400
http://www.gag.org

For information on membership, contact
Guild of Natural Science Illustrators
PO Box 652
Ben Franklin Station
Washington, DC 20044-0652
Tel: 301-309-1514
Email: gnsihome@his.com
http://www.gnsi.org

This national institution offers exhibits, lectures, educational programs, and social exchange with other illustrators.
Society of Illustrators
128 East 63rd Street
New York, NY 10021-7303
Tel: 212-838-2560
http://www.societyillustrators.org

and holiday pay. Freelance illustrators do not typically receive fringe benefits.

Outlook

Employment for artists is expected to grow about as fast as the average over the next several years. Employment will be even better for skilled illustrators as the print and electronic media and the film and video industries continue to expand.

There are few opportunities available in fashion illustration, since photography and film are more popular for magazines and catalogs.

The field of medical illustration is small, but the field of medicine and science in general is always growing, and medical illustrators will be needed to depict new techniques, procedures, and discoveries.

Marketing Research Analysts

What Marketing Research Analysts Do

When companies want to market a new product or improve an existing one, they often rely on market research to guide them. Market research is the process of collecting data about consumers, the marketplace, and the competition. *Marketing research analysts* collect, analyze, and interpret this information.

Marketing research analysts conduct several different types of research. Sometimes they investigate company products and services. Existing products are studied to see how they might be improved. Experimental products are examined to figure out how consumers might react to them or how these products might fare against their competition.

Marketing research analysts also investigate sales methods and policies. Sales figures are collected and studied. The researchers try to find out where a product is selling well and who is buying it.

Advertising is another area that marketing research analysts investigate. They try to determine the effectiveness of advertising for particular products or services by looking at sales figures.

Did You Know?

- The U.S. Census of 1790 is considered to be the first known survey conducted in the United States.

- Approximately 72 million people in the United States participate in opinion and marketing research studies each year.

- Approximately 135,000 marketing research analysts are employed in the United States.

Sources: Council of American Survey Research Organizations, Marketing Research Association, U.S. Department of Labor

A marketing research analyst discusses data with a colleague via the telephone. (Jim Craigmyle/Corbis)

Finally, marketing research analysts study consumer demands and opinions. For example, they explore what types of products consumers really want or why they prefer one brand over another.

There are five basic marketing research jobs. Some researchers work with statistics. They develop questionnaires and compile and analyze the results. Other researchers are *project supervisors*. They plan research studies and work with others to carry them out. The supervisor is also responsible for writing reports that contain the results of the studies. *Tabulators* and *coders* are the marketing research analysts who examine questionnaires when they come into the company's offices. They count the answers and write reports on the results. *Field interviewers* are researchers who actually interview consumers about their preferences, opinions, likes, and dislikes. *Telemarketers* are interviewers who gather information by placing calls to current or potential customers, to people listed in telephone books, or to those who appear on specialized lists obtained from list houses.

Education and Training

If you are interested in market research, take courses in English and social studies in high school. Because statistics play an important role in market research, you should also take

EXPLORING

○ Conduct your own market research about a computer game, type of food, or other item. Ask your friends and family their opinions about the item and record and tabulate their responses.

○ Experiments in science, problems in student government, committee work, and other school activities will provide you with exposure to situations similar to those encountered by marketing research analysts.

○ Talk to a marketing research analyst about his or her career.

To Be a Successful Marketing Research Analyst, You Should . . .

- be intelligent
- be detail oriented and accurate
- have the ability to work easily with words and numbers
- be particularly interested in solving problems involving data-collection and data-analysis processes
- have excellent communication skills, both oral and written

as many mathematics courses as possible. Other helpful classes are marketing, business, speech, journalism, psychology, and sociology. Computer science courses are especially useful, because marketing research involves a lot of calculating and analysis that is easily done by computers.

After high school, you should enroll at a college offering degrees in economics, math, marketing, statistics, or business administration. Most employers require their marketing research analysts to hold at least a bachelor's degree. Many companies prefer workers with master's degrees.

Earnings

Beginning salaries in marketing research depend on the qualifications of the employee, the nature of the position, and the size of the firm. Interviewers, coders, tabulators, and a variety of other employees usually get paid by the hour and may start at $6 or more per hour. The U.S. Department of Labor reports that median annual earnings of market research analysts were $54,670 in 2003. Salaries ranged from less than $30,360 to $102,450 or more. Experienced analysts working in supervisory positions at large firms can make even more money.

FOR MORE INFO

For profiles of advertising workers, career information, and trivia games, contact
Advertising Educational Foundation
220 East 42nd Street, Suite 3300
New York, NY 10017-5806
http://www.aded.org

For career resources, contact
American Marketing Association
311 South Wacker Drive, Suite 5800
Chicago, IL 60606
Tel: 800-262-1150
Email: info@ama.org
http://www.marketingpower.com

For information on marketing and public opinion research, contact
Council of American Survey Research Organizations
170 North Country Road, Suite 4
Port Jefferson, NY 11777
Tel: 631-928-6954
Email: casro@casro.org
http://www.casro.org

For information on marketing, contact
Marketing Research Association
1344 Silas Deane Highway, Suite 306
Rocky Hill, CT 06067-1342
Tel: 860-257-4008
Email: email@mra-net.org
http://www.mra-net.org

Outlook

Job growth for marketing research analysts will be faster than the average over the next 10 years. Increasing competition among producers of consumer goods and services and industrial products, combined with a growing awareness of the value of marketing research data, will contribute to opportunities in the field. Opportunities will be best for those with graduate degrees who seek employment in marketing research firms, advertising firms, financial services organizations, health care institutions, manufacturing firms producing consumer goods, and insurance companies.

Media Planners and Buyers

What Media Planners and Buyers Do

Within a media department, *media planners* gather information about the sizes and types of audiences that can be reached through each of the various media and about the cost of advertising in each medium. *Media buyers* purchase space in printed publications, on billboards and the Internet, and on radio or television stations. In addition to advertising and marketing agencies, media planners and buyers work for large companies such as film studios, television networks, and radio stations that purchase space or broadcast time.

Media planners determine target markets based on their clients' advertising needs. Through their research, planners identify target markets (in this case, parents, children, and so forth) by sorting data according to people's ages, incomes, marital status, interests, and leisure activities.

By knowing which groups of people watch certain shows, listen to specific radio stations, or read particular magazines or newspapers, media planners can help a television network, for

To Become a Successful Media Planner and Buyer, You Should . . .

- have a strong understanding of advertising, publishing, television, film, and radio industries
- be knowledgeable about consumer buying trends
- have good problem-solving abilities
- be creative
- have excellent oral, written, and analytical skills
- have the ability to handle multiple tasks

example, select air time or print space to reach the consumers most likely to watch a specific program. For example, Saturday morning cartoons attract children, while prime-time programs often draw family audiences. These would be excellent places to advertise the new family comedy since these groups make up a large segment of potential viewers.

Media buyers do the actual purchasing of the time on radio or television or the space in a newspaper or magazine in which an advertisement will run. In addition to tracking the time and space available for purchase, media buyers ensure that ads appear when and where they should, negotiate costs for ad placement, and calculate rates, usage, and budgets. They are also responsible for maintaining contact with clients, keeping them informed of all advertising-related developments, and resolving any conflicts that arise.

In contrast to print and broadcast planners and buyers, *interactive media specialists* are responsible for managing all critical aspects of their clients' online advertising campaigns. While interactive media planners may have responsibilities similar to those of print or broadcast planners, they also act as new technology specialists, placing and tracking all online ads and maintaining relationships with clients and webmasters alike.

EXPLORING

- ○ Choose a popular television or radio show and determine its target audience and the best advertising methods to reach this group of people.
- ○ Work as a production assistant, programmer, writer, or editor in your school's media department.
- ○ Work as an advertising salesperson for your school's yearbook or theater department.
- ○ Volunteer or work part time for the classified advertising department of your local newspaper.

Education and Training

Although most media positions, including those at the entry level, require a bachelor's degree, you can prepare for a future job as media planner and/or buyer by taking specific courses in high school. These include business, marketing, economics,

Words to Learn

advertisement paid announcement of a product or service to the public

advertising agency group of researchers, writers, artists, buyers of space and time, other specialists, and account executives who design and execute advertising programs for clients

electronic banners the Internet's equivalent of billboard advertising, which accounts for 80 percent of online ads

market research the study of consumer groups to determine personal interests and characteristics

media the avenues through which advertisers can place ads, including the Internet, television, radio, magazines, newspapers, and outdoor signs

target audience a group of consumers that is considered the most likely to purchase a product; also known as **target market**

time slot the specific time that a commercial will air on radio or television

advertising, radio and television, and film and video. General liberal arts classes such as English, communication, and journalism are also important, since media planners and buyers must be able to communicate clearly with both clients and coworkers. In addition, mathematics classes will give you the skills to work accurately with budgets and placement costs. Increasingly, media planners and buyers have college degrees, often with majors in advertising or marketing.

Earnings

Because media planners and buyers work for a variety of organizations across the country and abroad, earnings can vary greatly. Advertising sales agents who were employed by advertising or related industries had average annual earnings of $53,460 in 2003, according to the U.S. Department of Labor. Salaries for all advertising sales agents ranged from less than $19,920 to more than $87,360. Media directors can earn

FOR MORE INFO

For profiles of advertising workers, career information, and trivia games, contact
Advertising Educational Foundation
220 East 42nd Street, Suite 3300
New York, NY 10017-5806
http://www.aded.org

between $46,000 and $120,000 depending on the type of employer and the director's experience level.

Outlook

The employment outlook for media planners and buyers, like the outlook for the advertising industry itself, depends on the general health of the economy. When the economy thrives, companies produce an increasing number of goods and seek to promote them via newspapers, magazines, television, radio, the Internet, and various other media. Employment in the advertising industry is projected to grow faster than the average for all occupations.

Merchandise Displayers

What Merchandise Displayers Do

Merchandise displayers design and build displays for store windows, showcases, and floors. They are sometimes called *display workers, showcase trimmers,* and *window dressers.* Store displays must be artistic and attractive so that customers will want to buy the products.

Some merchandise displayers work in self-service stores, such as supermarkets. Because there are no salespeople, displays are very important in attracting the customer to buy products. In large retail stores there may be a staff of display specialists. These workers often use mannequins and other props for displaying apparel. Merchandise displayers also prepare product displays for trade shows, exhibitions, conventions, or festivals. They build installations such as booths and exhibits. They also install carpeting, drapes, and other decorations, including flags, banners, and lights, and arrange furniture and other accessories.

Displayers first develop an idea or theme that will highlight the merchandise and attract customers. Display workers use hammers, saws, spray guns, and other hand tools to build displays. They may use carpeting, wallpaper, and special lighting.

To Become a Successful Merchandise Displayer, You Should . . .

- be creative
- have manual dexterity and mechanical aptitude
- possess the strength and physical ability needed to carry equipment and climb ladders
- be agile in order to work in close quarters without upsetting the props
- have strong communication skills

EXPLORING

- ○ Observe merchandise displayers as they prepare a display in a department store window.
- ○ Help your neighbors arrange items for garage or yard sales.
- ○ You can find lots of opportunities to work on displays at school. Ask your teachers if you can help design and arrange bulletin boards, posters, or displays for special events, such as parents' night and fundraisers.
- ○ Participate in groups that are in charge of decorations or publicity for school dances and parties.
- ○ Join your school or community drama group to work on sets, props, and costumes.
- ○ Take art, sculpture, calligraphy, or carpentry courses offered in your community.

They build and paint the backdrops and gather all the props they'll need. Finally, they arrange merchandise and hang printed materials such as signs, descriptions of the merchandise, and price tags.

Sometimes display workers work in teams where each worker has a specialty, such as sign making, window painting, or carpentry.

Education and Training

Merchandise displayers must have at least a high school education. Courses in art, woodworking, mechanical drawing, and merchandising are useful. Some employers expect their merchandise displayers to have taken college courses in art, fashion merchandising, advertising, or interior decorating.

Art institutes, fashion merchandising schools, and some junior colleges offer courses in merchandise display. Many merchandise displayers receive their training on the job. They may start as sales clerks and learn while assisting window dressers or display workers.

Earnings

According to the U.S. Department of Labor, merchandise displayers employed in advertising and related services earned mean salaries of $22,210 in 2003. Merchandise displayers in all fields earned $14,710 or less, and more experienced displayers

A merchandise displayer sets up a clothing display in a department store window. (Paul A. Souders/Corbis)

Top Employers/Average Earnings for Merchandise Displayers

Employer	Employment	Average Earnings
Department Stores	11,000	$22,070
Advertising and Related Services	3,450	$22,210
Other Support Services	3,300	$29,940
Miscellaneous Nondurable Goods Merchant Wholesalers	3,310	$29,940

Source: U.S. Department of Labor

FOR MORE INFO

This organization offers information on becoming an interior designer, including school listings and details on career specialties.

American Society of Interior Designers
608 Massachusetts Avenue, NE
Washington, DC 20002
Tel: 202-546-3480
http://www.asid.org

To read about industry news and see the latest design ideas, check out the following magazine's website:

Display & Design Ideas
http://www.ddimagazine.com

earned $39,990 or more a year. Freelancers may earn as much as $50,000 a year, but their income depends on their reputation, number of clients, and number of hours they work. Display managers in urban areas earn more.

Outlook

The employment of display workers is expected to grow at an average rate. Retail businesses continue to grow and will need merchandisers to help sell products.

Photographers

What Photographers Do

Photographers take pictures to record events, illustrate text, sell products, capture scenes, and for many other purposes. They are experts on cameras, lenses, filters, film, and lighting. To prepare to take pictures, photographers choose the right film for the lighting conditions. They choose lenses such as a close-up lens or a wide-angle lens. They adjust all the settings on the camera so that the right amount of light hits the film for the right amount of time when the shutter button is pressed. These decisions are technical and require some mathematic ability, but they are also artistic decisions because small adjustments can give a great variety of special effects.

Photographers also know how to develop film and print pictures. They mix chemicals with precise measurements and soak the film in a series of mixtures for exact times. Once film is developed and dried, photographers place the film in enlargers that magnify the film. Lights in the enlarger shine through the film onto light-sensitive photographic paper. The paper is then soaked in a series of chemical baths, rinsed, and dried.

Photographers often specialize in one kind of photography. For example, *commercial photographers* take pictures of products, fashions, food, or machinery. *Scientific photographers* take pictures for scientific magazines

> **Top Magazines by Ad Pages, 2003**
>
> 1. *People*
> 2. *The New York Times Magazine*
> 3. *Bridal Guide*
> 4. *Forbes*
> 5. *Fortune*
>
> Source: Publishers Information Bureau

EXPLORING

○ Photography is a field that you can begin to explore now. Experiment with different cameras, films, and digital photography. Experiment with different kinds of pictures, too. Take photos of friends and family, school events, current events in your town, objects, landscapes, animals, or buildings.

○ Join school camera clubs or work on your yearbook or newspaper staff.

○ Enter contests sponsored by magazines or community groups.

○ You will find lots of photography resources in your library or bookstore and on the Internet. Look for information on how to compose photos, arrange lighting, determine camera settings, and choose film for various effects.

and books. *Photojournalists* take pictures of events, people, places, or things for newspapers, websites, and magazines. *Portrait photographers* take pictures of people in their own studios, or at schools, homes, weddings, and parties. *Aerial photographers* take pictures from airplanes for newspapers, businesses, research companies, or the military. *Fine art photographers* take pictures for artistic expression. They might shoot images that are beautiful, thought-provoking, or even disturbing to convey ideas and feelings.

Digital photography is a relatively new development. With this new technology, film is replaced by microchips that record pictures in digital format. Pictures can then be downloaded onto a computer's hard drive. Photographers use special software to manipulate the images on screen. Digital photography is used primarily for electronic publishing and advertising.

Education and Training

Classes in photography, chemistry, and art will help prepare you for this career. If you are interested in digital photography, study computers and learn how to use programs that manipulate photos.

You do not have to earn a college degree to become a photographer, but many colleges offer a bachelor's degree in photography. A college program will teach you advanced techniques and help you build a portfolio of your work.

Earnings

Photographers earned median salaries of $25,050 in 2003. Salaries ranged from less than $14,610 to $51,960 or more in 2003, according to the U.S. Department of Labor.

Many photographers are self-employed freelancers. Although they can take on a wider variety of assignments than most salaried photographers, their earnings can go up and down depending on how much work is available. In addition, self-employed photographers do not receive the benefits that a company provides its employees.

Outlook

Employment of photographers will increase about as fast as the average over the next several years. As more newspapers and

Top U.S. Advertisers, 2002 (by Spending)

1. General Motors Corp.
2. Time Warner
3. Procter & Gamble Co.
4. Pfizer
5. Ford Motor Co.
6. DaimlerChrysler
7. Walt Disney Co.
8. Johnson & Johnson
9. Sears, Roebuck & Co.
10. Unilever

Source: *Advertising Age*

magazines turn to electronic publishing, more photographers will be needed to provide digital images for advertisements and stories.

FOR MORE INFO

For information on careers in photography and education, contact
American Society of Media Photographers
150 North Second Street
Philadelphia, PA 19106
Tel: 215-451-2767
http://www.asmp.org

For information on training and their monthly magazine, contact
Professional Photographers of America
229 Peachtree Street, NE, Suite 2200
Atlanta, GA 30303
Tel: 800-786-6277
http://www.ppa.com

For information on student membership, contact
Student Photographic Society
229 Peachtree Street, NE, Suite 2200
Atlanta, GA 30303
Tel: 800-339-5451, ext. 237
Email: info@studentphoto.com
http://www.studentphoto.com

Photo Stylists

What Photo Stylists Do

Photo stylists work with photographers, art directors, models, and clients to create a visual image. They use props, backgrounds, accessories, food, linens, clothing, costumes, and other set elements to create these images. Much of the work they do is for catalogs and newspaper advertising. Stylists also work on films and television commercials.

Most stylists specialize in fashion, food, hair and makeup, or bridal styling. Some do only prop shopping or location searches. Others prefer to develop a variety of skills so they can find different kinds of photo styling work.

Photo stylists use their imagination, resourcefulness, and artistic skills to set up a shot that will help sell a product. For example, a mail-order clothing company may want a series of ads to sell their winter line of clothing. Photo stylists may decide to design a set outside with a snow background or indoors near a fireplace with holiday decorations in the background. They gather props such as lamps or table decorations. They rent chairs and couches to decorate the set where the shoot will take place. For an outdoor scene, they might use a sled or skiing

Styling Specialties

The following are some of the specialties in photo styling:

- beds and domestics
- bridal
- casting
- catalogs
- children
- fashion
- film, videos, and commercials
- food
- hair and makeup
- home furnishings
- illustration
- lifestyle
- locations
- production coordination
- props
- set design
- soft goods
- still life
- tabletop
- visual merchandising/display
- wardrobe

EXPLORING

○ Team up with friends and class-mates who are interested in pho-tography or film. Offer to help set up shots. A backyard photo shoot can be a good way to learn the ele-ments involved with this career.

○ Watch someone prepare a display in a department store window. Many stylists start out as window dressers.

○ Work on set design or props for a school or community theater.

○ Join a photography club and learn the basics of taking pictures. This will help you visualize what the photographer sees through the lens.

equipment. Photo stylists hire mod-els to wear clothing. They may work with other photo stylists and assis-tants to style the hair and makeup of the models.

Photo stylists usually have a "bag of tricks" that will solve problems or create certain visual effects. This kit may include everything from duct tape to cotton wadding to a spare salt shaker. Sometimes photo stylists build and design props from scratch. They may have to coordinate the entire production from finding the location to arranging accommoda-tions. The best photo stylists are ver-satile and creative enough to come up with ideas and solutions on the spot. If they cannot create or locate something, they have many contacts who can help them out.

Photo stylists must be organized. They must make sure to gather everything that they need for a photo shoot and be sure that all materials are well cared for. After the shoot, photo stylists make sure that all borrowed items are returned and that all rentals and other transactions have been recorded.

Education and Training

There is no specific training or schooling to become a photo stylist, but there are other ways to prepare for this job. Art classes can help train your eye for design and composition. Experience with building and constructing displays will be of great help. Sewing skills are necessary, especially in fashion photo design, where the stylist must often make minor alterations to fabrics. Those interested in hair and makeup styling should take courses in cosmetology. Interior design courses will help you arrange room settings. A general knowledge of photography, film, and lighting will help you communicate with photographers.

Most photo stylists enter the field as apprentices to established stylists. Apprentices usually work for two years or more before taking on clients on their own.

Earnings

Salaries at production houses can start as low as $8 an hour. Experienced fashion or food stylists can earn as much as $800 a day and more, depending on reputation and the budget of the production. On average, stylists earn around $350 to $500 per day as freelancers. According to the Association of Stylists and Coordinators, assistant photo stylists earn about $150 to $200 a day.

Styling Specialties

The following are some of the things photo stylists might carry with them to photo shoots:

- utility knife
- cloth steamer
- skewers
- toothpicks
- brushes
- cotton swabs
- tweezers
- glycerine
- oil
- spray bottles
- eye droppers
- blow torch
- mixer
- pastry bags and tips
- safety pins
- needle and thread
- tape

FOR MORE INFO

For more information about the work of photo stylists, contact
Association of Stylists and Coordinators
18 East 18th Street, Apt. 5E
New York, NY 10003
Email: info@stylistsasc.com
http://www.stylistsasc.com

For information on student membership, contact
Student Photographic Society
229 Peachtree Street, NE, Suite 2200
Atlanta, GA 30303
Tel: 800-339-5451, ext. 237
Email: info@studentphoto.com
http://www.studentphoto.com

Outlook

Employment of photo stylists is expected to grow at an average rate. Good photo stylists are becoming more and more important to photographers and advertising clients. However, the employment outlook of photo stylists depends on the health of the advertising, film, and commercial photography industries.

New digital photography and photo enhancement technology may change the role of the photo stylist in the future. There may be more educational programs for photo stylists and this may increase the competition for styling assignments.

Public Opinion Researchers

What Public Opinion Researchers Do

Public opinion researchers interview people in person, on the telephone, or through mailed questionnaires. Public opinion researchers are involved in selecting the questions to be asked, the people to be asked, asking the questions, and interpreting the results. They conduct these surveys to help business owners, politicians, and others determine how the public feels about certain issues, or what they like or dislike about selected products.

The method that researchers use depends on the type of information desired. For example, a shopping mall owner interested in determining why shoppers like to use the shopping center may have interviewers talk to shoppers as they go from store to store. An advertising executive interested in finding out what television programs people watch may have researchers call several thousand people at random and ask them about their viewing habits. Researchers not only talk to people in person or on the telephone, they also send out questionnaires and ask respondents to mail in their answers.

Planning is an important element of developing a questionnaire or other survey technique. Researchers decide what portion of the population they

> ### Advertising-Related Websites
>
> **Ad Track Index**
> http://www.usatoday.com/money/advertising/adtrack/index.htm
>
> **AdFlip**
> http://www.adflip.com

EXPLORING

○ Conduct basic public opinion research by asking your friends and family the same questions about a product, an issue in the news, or a popular movie or television show. You can compare their responses to get a basic idea of what public opinion researchers do every day.

○ If you are involved in student government, you may encounter issues that require a public opinion poll. Your teacher advisers can help you write fair, unbiased survey questions.

○ Working on your school newspaper also may give you opportunities to interview students, faculty, and parents about a variety of issues.

○ Ask your teacher to arrange a presentation by a public opinion researcher.

will survey and develop questions that do not force people to answer a certain way. Researchers often stay away from questions that allow only a yes or no answer so that respondents can express their feelings more fully.

Researchers who analyze the results often group people together according to age, geographic region, income, ethnicity, education, and other categories. For example, researchers may review all the answers of respondents between the ages of 30 and 45 to see how they feel about the selected topic. This type of grouping is very popular because it allows those who analyze a survey to suggest how other people with the same characteristics will feel about a topic. It also allows advertisers, politicians, and others to target their products, services, and messages to specific audiences.

Education and Training

Courses in English, speech, social studies, mathematics (especially statistics), journalism, and psychology are good preparation for this career. Knowledge of a foreign language is also helpful.

A college degree is not always necessary for those who conduct interviews, but researchers involved in developing questions and studying results should have at least a bachelor's degree in economics, business administration, sociology, or psychology. Those who study results need a good background

> ## Top U.S. Advertisers, 2002 (by Spending)
>
> 1. The Marlboro Man (cigarettes)
> 2. Ronald McDonald (fast food)
> 3. The Green Giant (frozen vegetables)
> 4. Betty Crocker (food products)
> 5. The Energizer Bunny (batteries)
>
> Source: *Advertising Age*

in statistics. Students who are interested in working in the advertising and marketing industries might want to minor in one of these areas in college. Because of the sophisticated techniques used by public opinion researchers, a familiarity with computers is expected, and a master's degree in business administration, sociology, educational psychology, or political science is often required.

Earnings

The U.S. Department of Labor reports that market research analysts (a type of public opinion researcher) earned median salaries of $54,670 in 2003. Earnings ranged from less than $30,360 to $102,450 or more. The department also reports that survey workers earned salaries in 2003 that ranged from less than $15,400 to $60,140 or more. The median annual salary for survey workers was $24,600 in 2003.

Outlook

Employment for market and survey research workers is expected to grow faster than the average over the next several years. Job opportunities should be excellent for people trained in public opinion research, particularly those with graduate degrees. People who specialize in marketing, mathematics, and statistics will have the best opportunities. Marketing research firms, advertising firms, financial services organizations, health care institutions, and insurance firms are potential employers.

FOR MORE INFO

For more information on market research, contact
Advertising Research Foundation
641 Lexington Avenue
New York, NY 10022
Tel: 212-751-5656
Email: info@thearf.org
http://www.arfsite.org

For information on market and public opinion research, contact
American Association for Public Opinion Research
PO Box 14263
Lenexa, KS 66285-4263
Tel: 913-310-0118
Email: AAPOR-info@goAMP.com
http://www.aapor.org

For comprehensive information on market and opinion research, contact
Council for Marketing and Opinion Research

1285 Silas Deane Highway, Box #123
Wethersfield, CT 06109
Tel: 860-571-6838
Email: info@cmor.org
http://www.cmor.org

For information on survey research and graduate programs, contact
Council of American Survey Research Organizations
170 North Country Road, Suite 4
Port Jefferson, NY 11777
Tel: 631-928-6954
Email: casro@casro.org
http://www.casro.org

For career information, contact
Marketing Research Association
1344 Silas Deane Highway, Suite 306
Rocky Hill, CT 06067-1342
Tel: 860-257-4008
Email: email@mra-net.org
http://www.mra-net.org

Public Relations Specialists

What Public Relations Specialists Do

When a company or an organization wants to present a good image to the public, it often turns to its public relations department or to a public relations firm. *Public relations specialists* include executives, writers, artists, and researchers. These specialists work together to provide information to the public about an organization's goals and accomplishments and about its future plans or projects.

Public relations specialists spend much of their time writing. They write reports, news releases, booklets, speeches, copy for radio and television, and film scripts. Public relations specialists also edit employee publications, newsletters, and reports to shareholders. All of this writing and editing has one goal: to offer the public positive information about a person or company.

Contact with the media is another important part of the public relations specialists' job. They use radio, television, newspapers, and magazines to communicate positive information about a client. They also use special

Museum of Public Relations Online

In late 1997, Spector & Associates introduced the Museum of Public Relations in cyberspace. The museum provides a history and examples of successful public relations programs for industry, education, and government through photographs and stories. There are also changing exhibits.

Check out the museum at http://www.prmuseum.com.

Source: *Communication World* Online, International Association of Business Communicators

EXPLORING

○ Almost any experience in working successfully with other people will help you to develop strong interpersonal skills, which are important in public relations.

○ Work as a volunteer on a political campaign to learn persuasive techniques.

○ Any teaching or speaking experience will help you learn how to organize a presentation and talk to a group of people.

○ Talk to a public relations specialist about his or her career.

events to get their messages across. Press parties, open houses, exhibits at conventions, and speeches help to establish good feelings and a positive image.

Some companies have their own public relations departments and hire their own workers. Other companies hire public relations firms whose workers provide public relations services to one or more companies. In either case, public relations specialists work closely with top executives to decide how to keep or improve a company's good image. Public relations workers sometimes do research or conduct public opinion polls. Then they develop a plan and put it into action.

Public relations specialists often meet with the media to provide information about their organization's goals and accomplishments. (Tom & Dee Ann McCarthy/Corbis)

Did You Know?

- More than 200 colleges and about 100 graduate schools offer degree programs or special courses in public relations.
- There are approximately 158,000 public relations specialists employed in the United States.
- Approximately 18,000 of these workers are employed in advertising or related services.
- Approximately 7 percent of public relations specialists are self-employed.

Source: U.S. Department of Labor

Education and Training

Most public relations specialists are college graduates. In high school you should take college-preparatory courses, especially English, speech, humanities, and languages. Writing is an important part of public relations, so you should build your writing skills, perhaps by working on school publications.

In college, you should pursue a degree in public relations, English, or journalism. Courses in creative writing, psychology, communications, advertising, and marketing, will also be useful. A graduate degree is often required for top managerial positions.

Some companies have training programs for newly hired public relations specialists. In other companies, new employees work closely under the supervision of a more experienced specialist. They read and file newspaper and magazine articles, research, and learn to write press releases.

The Public Relations Society of America and the International Association of Business Communicators offer accreditation to public relations workers. Although not required by employers, accreditation serves as a sign of competence in this field.

FOR MORE INFO

The following association publishes Communications World *magazine and provides other resource materials.*

International Association of Business Communicators
One Hallidie Plaza, Suite 600
San Francisco, CA 94102-2818
Tel: 415-544-4700
http://www.iabc.com

For statistics, salary surveys, and information on accreditation, contact
Public Relations Society of America
33 Maiden Lane, 11th Floor
New York, NY 10038-5150
Tel: 212-460-1400
http://www.prsa.org

Earnings

Public relations specialists employed in advertising and related services had mean annual earnings of $57,760 in 2003, according to the U.S. Department of Labor. Salaries for public relations specialists employed in all fields ranged from less than $25,050 to more than $77,830. Public relations managers may earn salaries that exceed $250,000 annually.

Outlook

Employment for public relations specialists is expected to increase faster than the average for all occupations over the next several years. Workers advance in this field quickly and move on to other jobs, and employers must replace them.

Most large companies have some sort of public relations resource, either through their own staff or through the use of outside consultants. They are expected to create many new jobs. More of the smaller companies are also hiring public relations specialists.

Telemarketers

What Telemarketers Do

Telemarketers make and receive phone calls for a company in order to sell goods, market services, gather information, receive orders and complaints, or handle other business. The activities telemarketers most frequently perform are inputting mail orders and verifying names and addresses. Telemarketing professionals might work directly for one company or for several companies that use the same telemarketing service.

Telemarketers generally work for one of two types of businesses. Some telemarketers are part of the in-house staff of a company and make and receive calls on behalf of that company. Others work for a telemarketing service agency and make or receive calls for the clients of the agency.

Telemarketers either handle incoming calls or place calls to outside parties. Incoming calls may include requests for information or orders for an advertised product, such as clothing, magazines, appliances, or books. Telemarketers also staff the phones that handle toll-free numbers that customers call to ask questions about the use of a product or to register complaints.

Telemarketers generally make outgoing calls to sell products and services

To Become a Successful Telemarketer, You Should . . .

- ○ be able to deal well with other people
- ○ be able to balance your company's concerns with the needs of the customer
- ○ have a warm, pleasant phone voice
- ○ be detail oriented
- ○ not mind sitting in one place for several hours
- ○ be able to have a conversation and use a computer at the same time

EXPLORING

- ○ Observe the different ways that businesses promote products or services on television, in stores, and in print. What sales techniques seem to be most effective? Which seem least effective and why?
- ○ Participate in a local fund-raising drive for a charity or non-profit organization.
- ○ Ask your teacher or parent to help you set up an interview with a telemarketer so you can find out about the day-to-day realities of their job.
- ○ Work on perfecting your speaking voice by recording yourself as you read aloud. Having a clear and friendly speaking voice is very important in a telemarketing career.

to consumers. The phone numbers that telemarketers call usually come from a prepared list of previous customers, reply cards from magazines, or a list purchased from another source. Once a sale is made, the telemarketer records all necessary information, such as the buyer's name and address, product choices, and payment information, so that order fillers can prepare the product for shipment.

Telemarketers also conduct marketing surveys to find out why people like and dislike a product or service. They may call to get people to vote for a candidate in an election or to tell citizens about an important vote in their city council. When making business-to-business calls, telemarketers may try to encourage attendance at important meetings, assist a company in recruitment and job placement, or collect demographic information for use in an advertising campaign.

Education

A high school diploma is usually required for any telemarketing position. Some employers hire only people who have earned a college degree. Since telemarketers sell and/or communicate over the telephone, they sometimes have college degrees in English, speech, drama, or communication. General business classes, such as marketing, advertising, and sales, are also good preparation for this career.

Earnings

Telemarketers' earnings vary with the type of work they do. The pay can range from the minimum wage ($5.15) to more than $17 per hour. As telemarketers gain experience and skills, their pay scales rise. Median annual earnings for telemarketers in 2003 were $19,870. Salaries ranged from less than $14,380 to more than $35,230.

Outlook

The Bureau of Labor Statistics expects telemarketer employment to decline through 2012. Causes for this decline may include the movement of call-center jobs overseas and the implementation of the National Do Not Call Registry. (See the

FOR MORE INFO

The AMA is an internal professional society of individual members with an interest in the practice, study, and teaching of marketing.

American Marketing Association (AMA)
311 South Wacker Drive, Suite 5800
Chicago, IL 60606
Tel: 800-262-1150
Email: info@ama.org
http://ama.org

For the Customer Service Newsletter *and other resources about customer service, contact*
Customer Service Group
28 West 25th Street, Eighth Floor
New York, NY 10010
Tel: 212-228-0246
Email: info@customerservicegroup.com
http://www.customerservicegroup.com

The DMA is the largest trade association for individuals interested in database marketing.

Direct Marketing Association (DMA)
1120 Avenue of the Americas
New York, NY 10036-6700
Tel: 212-768-7277
http://www.the-dma.org

The ATA is an industry advocacy group that offers professional education opportunities.
American Teleservices Association (ATA)
3815 River Crossing Parkway, Suite 20
Indianapolis, IN 46240
Phone: (317) 816-9336
Email: contact@ataconnect.org
http://www.ataconnect.org

The National Do Not Call Registry

Opened on June 27, 2003, the National Do Not Call Registry is a free service for people who wish to remove their phone number from telemarketers' call lists. By adding his or her number to the list, a person will receive a reduced number of telemarketer calls. One study found that consumers who added their numbers to the registry received an average of 30 telemarketing calls per month before registering; after registering they received only six per month. Telemarketers that call a number on the no-call list can be fined up to $11,000 per call.

sidebar on this topic.) Rapid growth and high turnover among workers will result in many opportunities for new people entering the telemarketing field.

Glossary

accredited   approved as meeting established standards for providing good training and education; this approval is usually given to a school or a program in a school by an independent organization of professionals

apprentice   person who is learning a trade by working under the supervision of a skilled worker; apprentices often receive classroom instruction in addition to their supervised practical experience

associate's degree   academic rank or title granted by a community or junior college or similar institution to graduates of a two-year program of education beyond high school

bachelor's degree   academic rank or title given to a person who has completed a four-year program of study at a college or university; also called an undergraduate degree or baccalaureate

career   occupation for which a worker receives training and has an opportunity for advancement

certified   approved as meeting established requirements for skill, knowledge, and experience in a particular field; people are certified by the organization of professionals in their field

college   higher education institution that is above the high school level

community college   public two-year college attended by students who do not usually live at the college; a graduate of a community college receives an associate's degree and may transfer to a four-year college or university to complete a bachelor's degree

diploma   certificate or document given by a school to show that a person has completed a course or has graduated from the school

distance education   type of educational program that allows students to take classes and complete their education by mail or the Internet

doctorate   highest academic rank or title granted by a graduate school to a person who has completed a two- to three-year program after having received a master's degree

fringe benefit   payment or benefit to an employee in addition to regular wages or salary; examples of fringe benefits include a pension, a paid vacation, and health or life insurance

graduate school   school that people may attend after they have received their bachelor's degree; people who complete an educational program at a graduate school earn a master's degree or a doctorate

intern   advanced student (usually one with at least some college training) who is employed in a job that is intended to provide supervised practical career experience

internship   (1) the position or job of an intern; (2) period of time when a person is an intern

junior college   two-year college that offers courses like those in the first half of a four-year college program; graduates of a junior college usually receive an associate's degree and may transfer to a four-year college or university to complete a bachelor's degree

liberal arts   subjects covered by college courses that develop broad general knowledge rather than specific occupational skills; the liberal arts are often considered to include philosophy, literature and the arts, history, language, and some courses in the social sciences and natural sciences

major (in college)   academic field in which a student specializes and receives a degree

master's degree   academic rank or title granted by a graduate school to a person who has completed a one- or two-year program after having received a bachelor's degree

online education   academic study that is performed by using a computer and the Internet

pension   amount of money paid regularly by an employer to a former employee after he or she retires from working

scholarship   gift of money to a student to help the student pay for further education

social studies   courses of study (such as civics, geography, and history) that deal with how human societies work

starting salary   salary paid to a newly hired employee; the starting salary is usually a smaller amount than is paid to a more experienced worker

technical college   private or public college offering two- or four-year programs in technical subjects; technical colleges offer courses in both general and technical subjects and award associate's degrees and bachelor's degrees

undergraduate   student at a college or university who has not yet received a degree

undergraduate degree   see bachelor's degree

union   organization whose members are workers in a particular industry or company; the union works to gain better wages, benefits, and working conditions for its members; also called a labor union or trade union

wage   money that is paid in return for work done, especially money paid on the basis of the number of hours or days worked

Index of Job Titles

Browse and Learn More

Books

Armstrong, Gary, and Philip Kotler. *Marketing: An Introduction*. 6th ed. Upper Saddle River, N.J.: Prentice Hall, 2002.

Berger, Warren. *Advertising Today*. Boston: Phaidon Press, 2001.

Pricken, Mario. *Creative Advertising: Ideas and Techniques from the World's Best Campaigns*. New York: Thames & Hudson, 2004.

Stair, Lila B., and Leslie Stair. *Careers In Marketing*. 3rd ed. New York: McGraw-Hill, 2001.

Sullivan, Luke. *Hey, Whipple, Squeeze This: A Guide to Creating Great Ads*. 2nd ed. Hoboken, N.J.: John Wiley and Sons, 2003.

———. *The WetFeet Insider Guide to Careers in Advertising and Public Relations*. San Francisco: WetFeet, 2003.

Wells, William, John Burnett, and Sandra E. Moriarty. *Advertising: Principles and Practice*. 6th ed. Upper Saddle River, N.J.: Prentice Hall, 2002.

Websites

About.com: Advertising
http://advertising.about.com

Advertising Age
http://www.adage.com

Advertising and Kids
http://dvlp.focusonyourchild.com/entertain/art1/A0000229.html

Advertising Educational Foundation
http://www.aded.org

Adweek
http://www.adweek.com

Brandweek
http://www.brandweek.com

Career Guide to Industries: **Advertising and Public Relations Services**
http://www.bls.gov/oco/cg/cgs030.htm

Emergence of Advertising in America: 1850–1920
http://scriptorium.lib.duke.edu/eaa

Marketing Research Association
http://www.mra-net.org

Museum of Advertising Icons
http://www.toymuseum.com

Museum of Public Relations
http://www.prmuseum.com